An Archive of Colours

Alyxander

ISBN: 9781723924057

To those forced a shoe that doesn't fit, to those with hands over their mouths and puppet strings above their heads. This is for you, I believe in you.

CONTENT

I

I am not the kind of person that can hide what they feel.
I'm what they call an open book.
You can feel my anger in the ground's shaking and the
waves' crashing. You'd hear the winds' whistling a little too
harshly, and see the clouds huddling over each other in
hurrying steps.
You can feel my calmness in the summer's breeze and in
the waves constantly visiting the shores.
You can feel my rare happiness in the most fleeting
moments; when the moon is twice its size for a change,
when the stars shine a little too brightly, when the flowers
first bloom after a harsh winter.
You can feel my sorrow the most; in the rain, in a flowers
withering, in the moons hiding.
What I feel makes me a force of nature. It holds power over
everything.

II

My days end out of tune and I can't ignore the beating of my heart.
Thud.
Thud.
Thud.
It's all I think about, all I see. I see it's shadow in the darkness around me. My block of cement heart makes my bed creak, scaring the souls away and makes my stirring room go rigid. All the colours in the air swaying to the tunes in their head stop to hear the beating. They stop to hear the thudding. All the thudding does is scare away. It scares away kind souls and bright colours. It scares away warm smiles and laughter from the stomach. It scares away my perception of self and my sense of home. It leaves me yearning for more.

III

In a peculiar state of mind. Never understanding the depth of the colours I'm drowning in. Never understanding how all this fear and rage is eating me alive. Looking for questions. Looking for answers. Looking for something. Courage, maybe? Warmth? Serenity? Looking for something. All the courage in me is to look you in the eye. All the warmth in me is mustered into a ball of fire and whirled your way. There is no serenity in me. Not for you at least. I know no gentleness. I tried sewing it on my skin, for you, I tried sewing it on my walls. It never worked, I only got wrath back. I got begging into a mirror for a feeling other than fear. I got asking questions to a mirror "am I withering?" "Are you growing?" "Am I a master? Or is that you?" I got tremours and blind sight when I needed the calmness of waves. I got the weight of the universe on my chest when I needed a spectrum of light.

IV

I'm with a new set of ghosts tonight.
They hear me whimper like a little boy and the
loneliness woven on my skin astounds them. The
drapes above me are the colour of love but my love
is nowhere to be seen. I'm with a new set of ghosts
tonight, they're too scared and appalled to make a
sound; the silence they bring makes my nights more
unbearable than they are. They speak in hushed
whispers and give me stares, foreign stares I am not
used to. I am used to their warm presence. To their
noisy steps. I got used to breathing easily in the
loud air, but for tonight, all I have is their heavy
silence.

V

This is a letter. This is a letter to anyone who ever came too close. This is a letter to apologise. I'm sorry if you ever tried to talk about a colour and how bright it got for you or a song that makes you feel on top of the world and I made you feel small. I'm sorry that sometimes I can't bear living in my burden of skin and I make you feel shades of dirt. Shades of blue or red. Shades of ugly. I'm sorry I can't contain myself sometimes, I'm sorry I hold the wrath of volcanoes and the grim of ravens. I'm sorry I'm nothing but a phantom when I long to be a stream of light.

VI

How do I casually bring up all the fear I carry everywhere with me? How do I casually bring up that I am a wretched soul who's looking for warmth? How do I casually bring up that all the toughness you see is but a shield I've built through my years of solitude? I am not strong, my love, but for you I try to be. I am nothing but the epitome of fear and cowardice, my sweet one, but for you I'm building a home. I'm nothing but a ghost with a withering soul, but for you the kiss of Death is hidden, and I am growing.

VII

Opening my eyes, seeing the sun outside, excitement
building up in me, rushing out of bed, running down the
silent stairs, the silent house. Knocking at your door with
sleep running after me, knocking at your door until you
answer. Opening the door for me with your warmest smile,
sleep is running after you too. Embracing me and flinging
me to the sky when I least expect it. That's the freest I ever
felt. Doing that on a daily basis, sometimes you don't
answer. Sometimes they tell me you didn't come home last
night. And when you did come back, you had a cast on your
leg, they said I can't bother you with nonsense any longer.
Never buying it, always looking for you everywhere. You're
sick, they said. Running whenever I hear laughter in the
silence. Running whenever I wake up with a smile on my
face. Running whenever the sun shines brighter. You're
getting better, they said.
They said that until one day they won't let me sit in the
house when it's silent. They'd lock the door so I don't go
running down the stairs.
Asking about you, missing you, you're away they said.
They said that whilst packing your things in boxes, putting
them away from clear sight. Sometimes they'd cry when I
ask or I'd get a stern look for bringing it up. Never bringing
it up again, I promised. Waiting for you every day,
sometimes outside your door.

They never told me what really happened until I got older.
You were napping, they said, you were napping and
someone important visited you. You couldn't say no, they
said, you just couldn't. You had to go with Him. You had to
go and come back another time, they said.

VIII

G,
I learned that you passed today, and it really surprised me. I never expect an immortal soul to go through that. You're too great to die. Was. Was too great to die. It's a real shame you passed, I was looking forward to more "agree to disagree" conversations. Time once again disappointed me.
I know for a fact I will see you in many things now. I will see you in Dostoevsky's work. I will see you in Nietzsche. I will see you in Moroccan prostitutes and red tea. I will see you in the last song I sent you.
I will miss you, and I hope you get this. we will meet again, in my next life, in a dream perhaps. It will happen.
I hope the universe is treating you better, wherever you are now. I hope the moon is listening to you. I hope the sun shines its soft rays on you. I don't think you know it, but you changed me. You left something that you should have taken with you, you left something that made all this harder. I drown in greys and purples and the brightest greens when I think of you, I really hope you're living your best life right now. With everything the way you want it. I can't wait to see you again.

IX

The house I live in is a ghost, and like ghosts, it carries all memories of lighter and pinker days on its ragged back. It reeks of nostalgia and dust. Every time I visit I see the house widening in my vision looking like the tower I thought it was when I was younger. Every time I visit I can see the broad windows sucking all the sunlight in, I can hear the clatter of dishes and chatter of grownups in the morning. Every time I visit I can smell the adventure of exploring every room and I can hear the laughter of my lost grandfather. Every time I visit I can smell the fear I had of the ghosts who lived in the abandoned floor, the ghosts who always tried to imbalance our sliding down the stairs. The ghosts who were always there to stop us when the grownups weren't.

X

You've snatched everything from my grasp- you've left me with nothing. You did it in such a convincing way; plucking away all that I am with sweet, sweet words. Before you, I was a galaxy that pleased your hungry sight. I was a nebulae illuminated by the stars in spectacular colour. I was a cluster of stars, a bundle of galaxies. But after you, you've twisted and crumpled all that's left. You turned me into a blackhole. Who would've thought such hefty actions would come out of my astrum. Everything I touch is fumbled into something less than a being, could it get any worse? You left me in swirls of the darkest colours and I can't get my head out of the clouds.

XI

Remember that time you came over and all we did was read?
Remember how cold the room was and how heavy the air felt with words?
Remember how we talked about good books and how they sucked the life out of you?
Remember? Oh and that conversation we had about space and I couldn't help but blurt out that you're a universe wrapped around itself? You always said that was the best thing someone ever told you.
But, love, how would someone you don't even give a second glance to say something that's that (the best thing someone ever told you)?
To me, you're so much more than that.
To me, you're the smell of books and feelings that can't be described.
To me, you're marvelous sunsets and engulfing darkness.
To me, you're a swirling star.
To me, you're a person filled with so much passion and destruction and isn't even aware of it; you're something extraordinary, and I can't wait to discover all parts of you.

XII

I long for you.
I long for your smell to consume my sheets and
your clothes to be scattered on my bedroom floor.
I long for your laughter to echo in my hollow self
and your breath to be the last thing I hear before
going to sleep. I long for your arms to be around
me; shielding me from every dreadful thing
happening. I long for nights filled with the melody
you call your voice and days filled with your holy
presence. I long to be touched by you, love, even
though everything you touch turns to ashes. Even
though every step I take closer to you combusts
whatever fire is left in me. Even though I seem to
be tied between loving and hating you with all my
might. Even though you get more confusing by
the day, love, I don't think I'll ever stop.

XIII

All my days are made up of more of less the same events, the same people. They lack the flavour of the stars or the sight of love. By the time I get to bed though, I like to think that's when the fun starts. The fun starts when the lights are out. The fun starts when I float on my bed like I have my back against the sea's waves. I float on my bed like I'm on a magic carpet among a soft breeze. I float on my bed and I think of you. I think of us. I float on my bed with souls all around me dropping my things and waking me up, and I think of our tongues clashing. I float on my bed and I get a sudden thought that sends chills down my spine but then I hear you whisper my name. I taste it on my lips. I float on my bed, in my dark, noisy room and I smile to myself. I tell the souls all about you.

XIV

Letters written to a flower, a purple flower to be exact.
Wondering if all there is to existing is hurting. Hurting and
healing. Do we disappear once we fully heal? Like scars do?
Or are we there glittering like ghosts going on with our
lives? Is being drenched in pink something that makes us
stand out or fade into the background?
I don't know if I have answers to any of that, all I know, is
that I'm willing to find out. I'm willing to beam and hold
my head up high. I'm willing to try.

XV

(I said I'll sleep but I want to write this down)
My sun,
I am someone who has looked Death in the eye far too
many times; waiting (and welcoming) its Kiss. It is only
after I met you, that I grew to fear it, most out of
anything. It is only now I long to live in different
colours with you, and because of you. It is only now I
rest my eyes and whisper to myself "this too shall pass".
It is only now I have hope brewed in all parts of me,
because of you, for you. It is only now I try to grab the
scurrying words coming out of my mouth, tucking them
back in and erasing the thought. It is only now, and only
you that truly matters.
I adore you far more than I am capable of.

XVI

You keep me grounded. My head has always been in the stars. My body has always floated in the cosmos, away from everything, with no sense of self. Now that I have you, my love, my thoughts don't stray away and I can make sense of all the tunes around me. Now that I have you, my body floats in colours and my hands are always stained in ink. Now that I have you, I always find myself orbiting back to you, I wouldn't want to have it any other way.

XVII

My darling,
My sleep has been deep these days, I always wake up too exhausted to start my day. My tired eyes are incapable of registering any colours; my blurry days are blending onto one another; my calloused hands are bleeding from the tumbling of my walls. I feel unfamiliar wherever I go, all I know, all I fathom, is how much I long for you. How much I miss you. I long for your warmth and all the yellows you make me feel. I long for eyes filled to the brim with love, your touch and all the pinks within your grasp. I long for every colour, every emotion you make me feel. I long for you, my precious one, the thought of seeing you again fills me with serenity and joy.

You complete me,
A.

XVIII

Love comes in every colour, they say, and I nod my head.
Love comes in red. In shades of passion and desire.
Love comes in orange. In shades of warmth and vitality.
Love comes in yellow. In shades of sunshine and joy.
Love comes in green. In shades of serenity and growth.
Love comes in blue. In shades of compassion and sorrow.
Love comes in indigo. In shades of harmony and spirituality.
Love comes in purple. In shades of longing and loss.

Love is alive and is everywhere. Love is love.

XIX

You've been dwelling recently. You've been thinking of
all the other shades you used to feel, thinking of the
deeper blues and vibrant reds. They haven't been
showing up as much as they used to. Everything is going
a lighter way now. Everything is messier, but now certain
shades of colour don't scare you anymore. Now, you can
look anything in the eye, you have your words and you
let them flow like breathing instead of keeping them in.
Now you're learning how to be kinder to yourself, and
you're there.
You used to drown in midnight blues like it was nothing.
You did it so much that you're now left with blue skin,
with a blue heart. That's okay though, it's okay that it's
there to remind you of where you've been and where you
are now. Now you try to drown in a new colour every
day. You go in pools of orange, pink, green, purple, and
yellow with your blue skin. You're proud of yourself.
I'm proud of you. I'm proud of you for being cozy in
your blue skin, and that it's not stopping you from
anything anymore.

Acknowledgements

I'm writing the acknowledgements for my book. *My book.* This feels surreal, and this is the outcome of the support and enthusiasm of many. To mention but a few; I want to thank my bumblebee, for your support, motivation, help, and inspiration. Thank you for being the angel that you are and for guiding me when I need it. Thank you for making my life lighter than I ever deemed it to be. I live for you. Thank you to the lovers, Axara and Sara, for making the cover of this book just as I imagined it. I am forever grateful to you. You can contact them at axara.sara0@gmail.com

Thank you, Pluto, for giving me the reassurance and support of the stars. What you have to say always matters more than others.

Thank you, Luna, for being an eminent ray of light. You mean so much to me.

Thank you to the loveliest vampire there is, for telling me how to describe certain colors and feelings perfectly.

Thank you, Valerie, for seeing things the way I see them, and for inspiring me.

Thank you to most English teachers I had during school and my continuing years in university, you've all been an inspiration.

I am here because of all of you, and because of you reading this. I hope you enjoyed reading this as much as I enjoyed making it.

Alyxander.

ABOUT THE AUTHOR

If you're looking for Alyxander, you will find him in the company of his ghost friends and the scent of love all around him. He spends most of his time watching or reading and talking to his lover and friends.

Do not hesitate to contact the author.

Twitter: @alyxander_n

E-mail: alyxander.n@gmail.com

12117387R00030

Printed in Great Britain
by Amazon